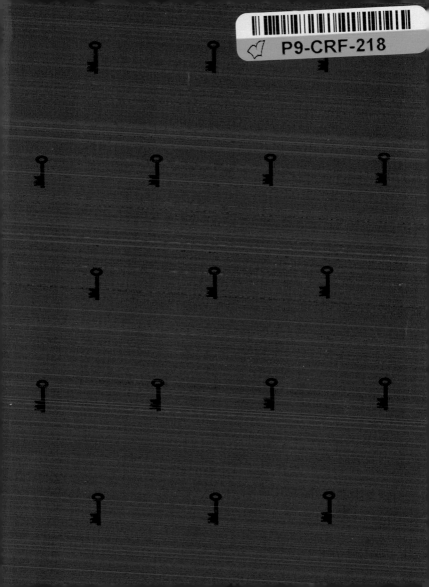

I hope you
always have
pleasant dreams

Brenda

love Kim

PROSPERO'S LIBRARY

The Book of
Dream Symbols

CHRONICLE BOOKS
SAN FRANCISCO

First published in the United States in 1995 by Chronicle Books.

A DBP Book, conceived, edited and designed by
Duncan Baird Publishers
6th Floor
Castle House
75–76 Wells Street
London W1P 3RE

Text: *Peter Bently*
Design: *Karen Wilks*
Commissioned artwork/photography:
Nick Bell, Ian Craig, Peter Crowther, Richard Jenkins, Sheena Land,
Emma Parker, Paul Redgrave, Peter Till, Steve Wallace
See page 40

Library of Congress Cataloging-in-Publication Data available

ISBN 0-8118-0664-2

Distributed in Canada by
Raincoast Books
8680 Cambie Street
Vancouver, B.C., V6P 6M9

10 9 8 7 6 5 4 3

Chronicle Books
85 Second Street
San Francisco, CA 94105

Printed in Hong Kong

Contents

The universal language

The stuff of dreams 4
The archetypes 6
The whole self 8
Metamorphoses 10
The self and others 12

Dreams of the real self

Love and passion 14
Hope and ambition 16
Dangers and demons 18
The dreamer in motion 20
Omen and prophecy 22
Children's dreams 24

The landscape of dreams

Nature 26
Flame and flood 28
Buildings 30
Travel and transport 32
Pursuit and capture 34
The body 36
Clothing 38

Acknowledgments 40

The stuff of dreams

The psychoanalyst Sigmund Freud (1856-1939) said that to unlock the secret symbolism of our dreams we need look no further than ourselves. Filtered through the unconscious, our most profound experiences are presented back to us in scrambled form.

Distortions

The size of things in dreams will often be determined by factors such as their importance in our lives. We may dwarf the world around us (a possible indication of egocentricity); or everyday objects may become terrifyingly huge, as they seemed in childhood.

Time and space

In a few seconds of dreaming we can live through hours, weeks, years or a lifetime. A dream may take us backward or forward in time to encounter ancestors, historical figures, our younger or older selves, even unborn generations. Locations can also shift abruptly, transporting us from the comfort of a familiar room to some foreign city or dizzy mountain precipice.

Mutations
Dreams happily ignore the laws of
nature. Solid walls yield to the touch,
stairs and floors become soft like sand,
animals walk or talk as we do. Curious
hybrids of humans and animals populate
the dream world: one theory
suggests that dreams may
be the source of ancient
deities such as the
dog headed Egyptian
divinity Anubis.

The archetypes

Freud's pupil Carl Gustav Jung (1875-1961) identified a number of archetypes, or "structural elements of the psyche". These are the basic ingredients of the unconscious, symbolized in dreams by various images drawn from the conscious world.

Animus and anima

The animus, the male side of the female persona, represents "masculine" qualities, such as courage and rationality. In dreams it could be symbolized by a white knight or by a modern counterpart such as a detective hero. The anima, the female side of the male persona, represents "female" qualities, such as compassion and emotionality. In dreams it may appear as a mother figure or as a powerful personality, such as the biblical Judith.

Great Mother and Wise Old Man

The Great Mother is the entirety of the
female persona. Its aspects include the
"Angry Goddess" (possessive and
destructive), the "Princess" (warm
and loving) and the "Amazon"
(intellectual and ambitious). The

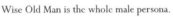

Wise Old Man is the whole male persona.
Its aspects include the "Ogre" (authoritarian
and conformist), the "Hero" (aggressive
and strong-willed) and the "Trickster"
(unpredictable and elusive) (above).

Shadow

Deep in the unconscious lurks the Shadow,
the dark side of the conscious persona. It may
be alarming for the dreamer to encounter a cruel,
self-centred alter ego. But we are all capable of
evil: to recognize this makes it less likely that
the Shadow will torment us with its
repressed urges.

The whole self

Jung defined the Self as "the totality of the psyche". Encompassing the dreamer's entire personality, it comprises both conscious and subconscious minds. The Self is symbolized in dreams in many forms: one is the *mandala*, a geometrical emblem containing a distinct focal point, like the device used for meditation in Eastern mysticism.

Mirror

Meeting our reflection in a mirror suggests a desire to see ourselves as others do, perhaps as part of a broader search for self-knowledge. It also warns about pushing the search too far: beware of narcissism!

Hail, myself

An encounter with one's *doppelgänger,* or double,
is traditionally held to be an omen of death;
in dreams it is likely to reveal an awareness
of mortality. Meeting yourself as a baby
or child suggests a desire for the security
of early years, while a meeting with
the aged self may express deep-seated
worries for the future. A *doppelgänger*
who behaves in an uncharacteristically
menacing way probably represents
the dreamer's Shadow, or sinister
alter ego.

Pole

The North and South Poles define the
axis around which the world revolves,
just as the Self is the axis of the dreamer's
persona. Searching for the pole
in a dream implies a quest for
the true focal point of the
personality, the starting point
for its future development.

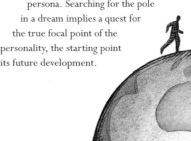

Metamorphoses

Since ancient times, shape-changing has had a powerful hold on the imagination. A dream metamorphosis may reveal basic aspects of the Self: for example, the dreamer may turn into a creature or person showing characteristics of one of the Jungian archetypes.

Wild beast

If the dreamer becomes a powerful animal, such as a lion, tiger or bull, this may reflect a struggle to get inside (and thereby overcome) what Jung called "the animal instincts of the unconscious". Or it could indicate a subconscious fear of one's own raw physical power, especially within a sexual relationship.

Role-playing

Transformation into another person can reveal much about our self-image. For example, to become an actor or actress suggests a suspicion that we are not presenting our true face to the world. Cleopatra may represent the archetype of the Great Mother, while Shakespeare could stand for the Wise Old Man — although such important historical figures could also indicate that the dreamer is prey to egotism.

The self and others

Dreams reveal how, from the earliest age, other people have defined our individuality. The relationship of child, mother and father is the most fundamental influence on the formation of the Self. The anonymous mass of fellow humanity is another powerful shaping force.

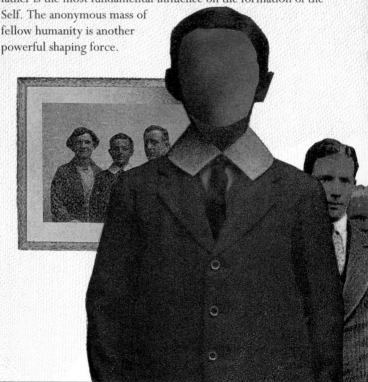

Family

Members of the family usually stand for themselves or for the attributes they represent and have helped to shape in the dreamer, such as motherhood. If the whole family appears, the dreamer may be trying to shake off the influence of father, mother or a sibling by submerging him or her in the wider group.

Ancestors

If ancestors appear in a dream, this may reflect a search for higher moral or spiritual values, especially if the dreamer assumes an ancestor's identity. Such dreams may also reveal an attempt to probe as deeply as possible into the recesses of the Self, in search of what Jung called our "innate psychic disposition".

Crowds

If, in a dream, we see ourselves as part of a great throng, this may indicate a desire to assume a more anonymous role in life, shaking off worries and responsibilities that have become too great a burden. If everyone is staring at us, we may be worried about making a bad impression on others.

Love and passion

Freud never believed, as is popularly supposed, that all dreams have a sexual content. However, he did claim that love and sex lay at the root of much dream symbolism and asserted that any idea or image was capable of representing the dreamer's erotic behaviour and desires.

Fruit
The apple is associated with the classical love goddess Venus and with Eve's temptation of Adam. In dreams, apples can also represent breasts and hence the dreamer's mother. Peaches and similarly shaped fruit represent the female genitalia.

Fish
The fish, an ancient and highly potent symbol, is associated with the depths of the unconscious. In dreams a fish may reflect a man's sexual urges or a fear that he will lose his virility.

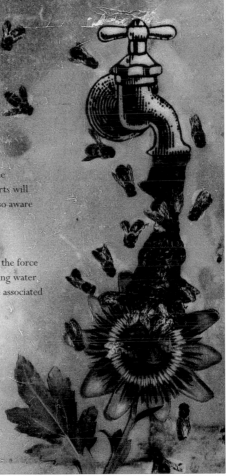

Bees

These restless insects, linked with love and fertility since ancient times, express both the aspirations and the doubts of the dreamer in love. We hope our efforts will bring sweet results – but we are also aware that we might be stung.

Running water

Water in general is associated with the force of life and generative power. Gushing water is said to denote the sense of release associated with orgasm.

Flowers

A common emblem of blossoming or, if the flowers are withered, declining love. Fallen petals may symbolize the dreamer's feelings about the prospect (or reality) of losing his or her virginity.

Hope and ambition

Dreams reveal our most deeply felt aims and aspirations. A race may symbolize the urgency with which we wish to see our goals fulfilled. Walls can stand for obstacles that threaten to thwart our ambitions. Symbols such as the Holy Grail, the cup or bowl used by Christ at the Last Supper, point to hopes and yearnings of the highest spiritual kind.

Rainbow
According to the ancient dream writers, rainbows presage good fortune. However, they are believed today to contain a possible warning against overambition. Jung wrote: "Only the gods can walk rainbow bridges in safety … for the rainbow is just a lovely semblance which spans the sky, and not a highway for human beings."

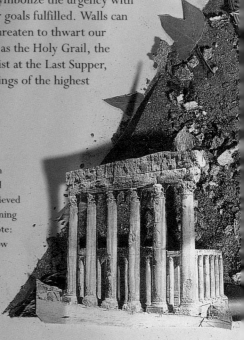

Heavenly ladder

The ladder between the earth and the heavens expresses the dreamer's aspirations to a higher level of spiritual or material attainment. In the Bible, Jacob dreams of a stairway to Heaven; from the top of it God promises Jacob that his descendants will inherit the land of Israel.

Gold

Alchemists spent centuries searching in vain for the mystical "philosopher's stone" that would turn base metals into precious gold. Gold symbolizes the dreamer's highest material aspirations, with the implication that they might be unattainable.

Temple

Temples and other places of worship are often designed as microcosms – that is, miniature representations of the cosmos. In dreams, they can symbolize the pursuit and achievement of creative and spiritual goals.

Dangers and demons

Behind the closed doors of the mind lurk the dark forces that encroach upon the dreamer's hopes and happiness. Dreams can open these doors, presenting anxieties and uncertainties as concrete images from the waking world. For example, a pirate or other disreputable figure may symbolize the suppressed guilt assailing the dreamer's conscience.

Unknown waters

Seas and lakes may represent the unfathomed depths of the mind, where our anxieties and untested capacity for evil lie hidden. Freud, though, believed that water often symbolizes a craving for the safety of the womb.

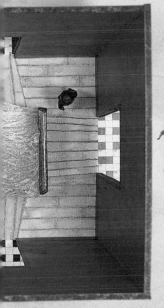

Vampires

The bloodsucking demon that takes the form of a bat to feed on the sleeping victim may represent fear or guilt in the face of excessive or illicit (even incestuous) sexual desires.

Horned creatures

Beasts with horns, such as goats, bulls or even horned beetles, were once linked with the sinister side of phallic power, as embodied in figures such as the Devil and the Greek god Pan. However, in modern times these creatures may be seen to represent male sexual potency as a positive, creative force.

Sharpened weapons

Knives, swords or other blades could be a warning of suicidal tendencies or a secret death wish toward someone else. For the older dream writers, these symbols meant that death, deceit, indifference or misunderstanding threatened to cut off close friends or loved ones.

The dreamer in motion

Dreams of unusual
activity, such as floating
in mid-air, can express
our innermost feelings.
The ancients recognized
the import of such dreams:
Artemidorus of Daldis claimed
that trying to run but being unable
to move meant that "your goals would
be hard to achieve".

Glued to the spot

Striving to run but getting nowhere could represent
an attempt to flee some powerful inner urge. The
dreamer may harbour secret desires but be
restrained by fear or shame from pursuing them.

Flying

Dreams of levitation are the
ultimate expression of a desire to leave
the earthly routine and be as free as a bird.
They could also denote soaring ambition.

Falling

To dream of falling is said to be a sign of anxiety
and vulnerability or an omen of misfortune.
This dream can also represent
yielding to the control of
another: for example, it may
symbolize sexual intercourse.

Landing

The earth is a symbol of fertility
and therefore of coupling – so hitting
the ground points to worries about a sexual
relationship. A soft landing (for example, on
flowers) indicates optimism about the outcome;
a hard landing, the opposite.

Omen and prophecy

A few days before his murder, Abraham Lincoln dreamed that the White House was in mourning for an assassinated president. Given proven cases such as this, it is understandable that modern psychology has not eradicated the traditional belief in the prophetic power of dreams.

The shower of fortune

A gentle or sudden shower is said by some writers on dreams to ensure prosperity in business and good fortune at sea. Rain may also signal an end to a barren period in the dreamer's intellectual or emotional life.

Birds of ill omen

Crows, rooks and ravens are usually said to be omens of bad luck or death. However, one English writer on dreams, Thomas Tryon (1634-1703), claimed that crows were harbingers of success in business.

Cats

The black cat is a herald of misfortune (although in English folklore it may be a lucky sign). A modern interpretation of its appearance in dreams is that the dreamer is on the verge of depression. White or silver creatures are generally considered to foretell good fortune. However, a white animal alongside a black one of the same species suggests a struggle for dominance between the light and dark sides of the Self.

Dreams of the real self

Children's dreams

Because children do not have an adult's grasp of
language and imagery it is not always easy to interpret their
accounts of their own dreams. However, a child's dreams tend
to reflect the jumble of new impressions that a young person
encounters each day on the path to knowledge and self-awareness.

Families
Bold geometrical shapes suggest a preoccupation with certain relationships within
the family, such as the triangle of father, mother and child. There is no need to
be too alarmed at violence done to a parent
in an older child's dream: the child is
probably overdramatizing a growing
need for independence.

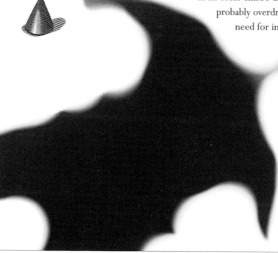

Teacher
A male teacher
represents male
authority and may
reflect the child's
concern about
its relationship
with its father,
especially if
the teacher
resembles
the parent.

Land of the giants

A child's impression of its size can reflect its sense of self-worth. Everything naturally seems bigger to a child than it does to an adult; but if a child takes on giant proportions in comparison with the surrounding world, its self-awareness could be increasing at a precocious rate.

Toys

A child's toys can come startlingly to life during sleep as the child lives out its fantasies. Some toys could denote developing aspects of the young dreamer's persona: a doll, for example, may symbolize a girl's growing sense of her own femininity.

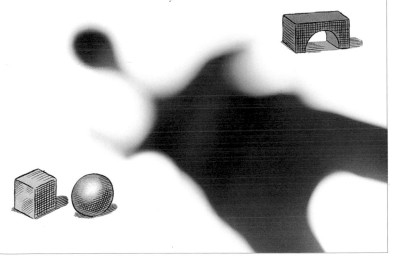

The landscape of dreams

Nature

The landscape furnishes dreams with powerful metaphors for the body and various aspects of the psyche. A spring can symbolize the fount of life and therefore the focus of the inner Self. A ploughed field could stand for motherhood and an uncut meadow for virginity. A deep valley may represent the womb.

Mountains

Life's challenges can present them-selves in dreams as hills and mountains: the steeper the slope, the greater the challenge. As early as c.350AD, the Greek writer Astrampsychus claimed that "to creep up a mountain signifies the difficulties of business".

Rivers

A river symbolizes life and the development of the Self. From small beginnings in the womb of the earth, it runs through many twists, meanders, torrents, falls and shallows, growing broader, deeper and slower as it approaches the end of its course.

Lakes

A secluded lake may represent some aspect of our persona we are seeking to learn more about. If, in a dream, a river flows into a lake, we could be trying to grasp what lies beyond the natural course of our lives.

Gardens

A symbol of the inner life and the qualities the dreamer may be cultivating, a garden can also be a *mandala*, or geometrical emblem of the Self, especially if it is enclosed and contains a focal point such as a fountain.

Trees

The tree is an ancient emblem of life and growth. It is also a phallic symbol and in a man's dream may reflect concerns about sexual or physical potency. In the Book of Daniel, the King of Babylon recounts one such dream: "an holy one came down from heaven; He cried aloud ... 'Hew down the tree, and cut off his branches.' "

Flame and flood

Fire and water, two of
nature's four elements, tend
to represent powerful forces
within ourselves, such as sexual
drive or maternal instincts.
Because they are irreconcilable
– fire evaporates water and
water extinguishes flame –
both elements occurring
in the same dream may
reflect some
great inner
conflict.

Fire

Fire is the heat of passion and lust,
and a blaze raging out of control
expresses our emotions at their most
unpredictable and destructive. In a
dream, our decision to fight or flee a
conflagration could reveal our ability or inability to confront our most extreme
feelings. But fire also means light, warmth and security (the hearth) and can be a
purifying force that clears out dead wood, opens new vistas and lights the way
through the dark forests of life.

Water

Dreams of deep, murky and turbulent
waters may represent the unconscious,
unformed Self on which our conscious
persona rests. Like fire, water stands
for the destructive forces within us –
as in dreams of devastating floods –
but it can also be a cleansing, purifying
element. Rivers are symbols of the
peaceful flow of life toward some
material or inner goal. Immersion may
symbolize a desire for a return to the
womb or for spiritual renewal.

Buildings

As the body is sometimes referred to as a house for the soul, so a house or other building can stand for the dreamer: behind the public façade of the outer persona are the dark, unexplored closets and secret chambers of the mind. The style of architecture may say something about our basic attitudes, from the moral stolidity of Victorian to the unrestrained exuberance of Baroque.

Basements and cellars

Jung had a dream in which he descended deeper and deeper into the basement of his family home, discovering a series of cellars, each more ancient than the last. The dream, he concluded, was an odyssey through the many layers of experience that made up his conscious persona.

Doorways and entrances

Freud said that, for some dreamers, a door or other
entrance "stands for one of the bodily orifices". But while
the act of passing through a door and into a hallway may be
open to sexual interpretation, it could also suggest that the
way out of some personal difficulty lies close before us.

Windows

In a dream, a window may have similar symbolism to a
doorway; however, it can also be a way of recognizing
our true outlook on the world. A pessimistic dreamer
might look through a window onto a bleak and barren
landscape, whereas an optimist might find the view bright
and verdant. Windows are also the means by which light
may be shed on our unconscious anxieties and aspirations.

Stairs and ladders

According to Jung, climbing steps
and ladders hints at "the process
of psychic transformation, with all
its ups and downs". Ascent indicates a yearning to reach a
higher plane of consciousness, while descent may point
to a quest for the unconscious. The regular motion of
climbing stairs or ascending and descending in an
elevator can stand for the sexual act.

Travel and transport

Dreams of undertaking a
long journey by land, sea or
air are often said to represent
a review of the dreamer's life
and goals. The hazards or crises
we encounter on the way through
life can appear as collisions,
breakdowns or barriers, while
dream destinations may
symbolize our aims
and achievements.

Road travel

Roads, with their twists, turns, forks
and crossroads, commonly represent
the journey through life, while
a horse or motor vehicle can
symbolize our energy and
motivation. If we are a passenger,
we may harbour a deep-seated sense
of being propelled through life by forces
of which we are not fully in command.

Aircraft

Dreams of air travel suggest
a desire for a direct, smooth
journey through life or some current
difficulty. If the dreamer is the pilot,
he or she is probably determined to be at
the controls of destiny. An air crash should
be heeded as a warning against overambition.

Trains

The raw power of the locomotive symbolizes
vitality, and the fixed track suggests the single-
minded pursuit of ambition. Missing a train
reflects a fear of missed opportunities or of
failure, while an attempt to alight from
a speeding train points to a desire to
take the pace of life a little easier.

Ships

The ship represents not just the dreamer's earthly career
but also the greater journey toward spiritual fulfilment.
Jung believed that ships could be vessels bearing the
dreamer over the depths of the unconscious.

Pursuit and capture

Dreams of flight and entrapment can tell us much about the most pressing concerns of our psychic lives, as in the case of the man who could not shake off his mother's influence and dreamed that he was a swimmer being pursued by a great sailing ship. The message of such dreams is that there is one thing we can never escape from: ourselves.

Hunter and hunted

Being pursued by some creature suggests a preoccupation that refuses to go away — perhaps because we do not really want it to. If the dreamer is being followed but feels no threat, this could indicate a deep-seated desire to attract more attention or affection.

Spider's web

A cobweb is both the spider's home and a deadly trap: hence, the dreamer may be feeling pushed into a domestic arrangement (perhaps marriage). A spider can also represent fate spinning the thread of destiny.

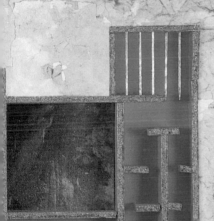

Maze

The maze can be a classic symbol of the Self. If we find ourselves inside one, we may need to consider which psychological direction we are taking. At the centre of the maze (the heart of the Self) lies either repose or – as in the Labyrinth of Greek myth, the lair of the monstrous Minotaur – dark, subversive forces.

Prison

A dream of being in custody may express a sense of sexual or emotional repression. It could also suggest that the dreamer has a guilty conscience – an interpretation accepted by both ancient and modern dream analysts.

No way out

A path leading to a cul-de-sac or blind alley may be a recognition that some current concern is leading nowhere: we should pursue a more viable course. If we are being chased and find ourselves with no escape route, it could be time to terminate an obsession before it overpowers us.

The body

As the outer framework of the inner self, the human body yields a wealth of fundamental dream symbols. These may throw light on what Jung called "the inter-functioning of body and psyche", one of the keys to self-awareness.

Hair
Hair is associated with the head as a centre of spiritual power. It is also a symbol of sexual potency, so a man who dreams of going bald may fear loss of virility.

Eye
Believed in the ancient world to be the window of the soul, the eye symbolizes the mind and the light of understanding. Something stuck in the eye may represent sexual intercourse.

Skeleton
The skeleton is a traditional symbol of mortality but it can also denote spiritual liberation and renewal – the death of a barren phase of life.

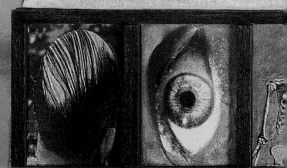

Hand

Hands may denote creativity, though the left hand could refer
to the dreamer's Shadow, or sinister, destructive urges. Dirty
hands suggest feelings of guilt.

Teeth

In dreams, becoming toothless can reflect worries about
the next phase of our lives and our strength to cope with
its challenges and responsibilities. A man who loses his teeth
may also fear castration, while a woman who swallows
hers may be contemplating motherhood.

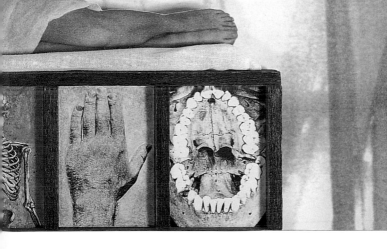

Clothing

In dreams, clothes reveal how we truly see ourselves or our role in life: someone who dreams of wearing an elaborate headdress may have a secret lust for power. Stripped of our clothes, all our vulnerability comes to the surface — as anyone knows who has had the common dream of being naked in public.

Hats

Freud and others perceived the hat as a classic symbol of the genitals. Whether the male or female parts are meant depends on whether the outside or the inside of the hat is more prominent in the dream.

Uniforms

Being uniformed in a dream may reveal a tendency to be influenced too much by the views of others, at the expense of one's own personality.

Shoes

The dreamer could be contemplating the next step in life. Shoes could also be a hint about being realistic in one's goals — keep both feet on the ground.

Glasses

Glasses express a desire to see things clearly. If one of the lenses is broken, the dreamer is said to be undergoing some inner conflict.

Veil

A veil implies that some aspect of the person is not being fully revealed, either to the dreamer or to the outside world.

Coat or cloak

An overcoat or cloak suggests a need for warmth, security and protection, either from a loved one or from God. Analyzing one of his patients, Freud saw a coat as a symbol of protected intercourse and, indirectly, worries about pregnancy.

Clothes too short

This suggests a yearning for the innocence of childhood or for old pleasures now curtailed.

Commissioned artwork and photography

Nick Bell – The whole self 8-9

Buildings 30-31

Ian Craig – Hope and ambition 16-17

Flame and flood 28-29

Travel and transport 32-33

Peter Crowther – Metamorphoses 10-11

Nature 26-27

Richard Jenkins – The body 36-37

Clothing 38-39

Sheena Land – Children's dreams 24-25

Emma Parker – Love and passion 14-15

The dreamer in motion 20-21

Omen and prophecy 22-23

Paul Redgrave – The stuff of dreams 4-5

The archetypes 6-7

The self and others 12-13

Peter Till – Title page and pages 7 (Trickster),

9 (Pole), 11 (Shakespeare),

24-25 (Toys), 30 (Stairs), 39

(Clothes too short)

Steve Wallace – Dangers and demons 18-19

Pursuit and capture 34-35